Joy & Pain
Life In The Key of Me

Joy & Pain
Life In The Key of Me

BY

TRACY WILSON

http://beautifulpublications.com

Published by
Beautiful Publications LLC
Stratford, CT 06614

This book is a compilation of songs written by me over the last 20 years. Some of the songs have been written into books already published by me, and some of them are waiting to be written into books published by me.

©Copyright 2020 Tracy Wilson

All rights reserved. No part of this publication may be reproduced or transmitted in any form or by any means, electronic or mechanical, including photocopy, recording, or any information storage and retrieval system, without permission in writing from the copyright owner, except by a reviewer who may quote brief passages in a review.

PRINT ISBN: 978-1-7356620-0-8
EBOOK ISBN: 978-1-7356620-1-5

Printed in the United States of America

Joy & Pain – Life In The Key of Me

VERSE	The way I feel for him should be no surprise. I know what he sees when he looks in my eyes. I look at him now and I see today, that something I'm sure of is coming my way...
CHORUS	And He Loves Me! And He Loves Me! And He Loves Me! And He Loves Me!
CHANGE	Now though, it seems the man of my dreams, finally sees just what I see, knowing for sure that we can be happy and free eternally.

CHANGE   Growing together – closer each day. Love is forever – we've found a way...

CHORUS   And He Loves Me!
          And He Loves Me!
          And He Loves Me!
          And He Loves Me!

VERSE   He feels for me now what I've felt for so long. I know what we have here could never be wrong. I love him so much now I don't feel the same, I've nothing to lose and everything to gain...

CHORUS   And He Loves Me!
          And He Loves Me!
          And He Loves Me!
          And He Loves Me!

My friend Theresa liked this song – she said it reminded her of country music.

Joy & Pain – Life In The Key of Me

VERSE	Was there ever a time when I wasn't there and you needed me? It isn't so... oh no...
	Was there ever a time when you needed to talk and you couldn't find me? It isn't so... oh no...
CHANGE	'Cause I'll always be there to show how much I care when you need me to help you, and if ever you feel that no one understands, then you'll know just what to do...

CHORUS	Call me up and tell me you need me tonight... Call me up and I will help you make things right... Call me up – I'll listen 'till you feel all right... Call me up...
VERSE	Is there ever a time when you feel so alone you can't come to me? It isn't so... oh no...
	Is there ever a time when you're feeling so down you don't want to see me? It isn't so... oh no...
CHANGE	'Cause I'll always be there to show how much I care when you need me to help you, and if ever you feel that no one understands, then you'll know just what to do...
CHORUS	Call me up and tell me you need me tonight... Call me up and I will help you make things right... Call me up – I'll listen 'till you feel all right... Call me up...

This was one of my Aunt Crystal's favorite songs.

Joy & Pain – Life In The Key of Me

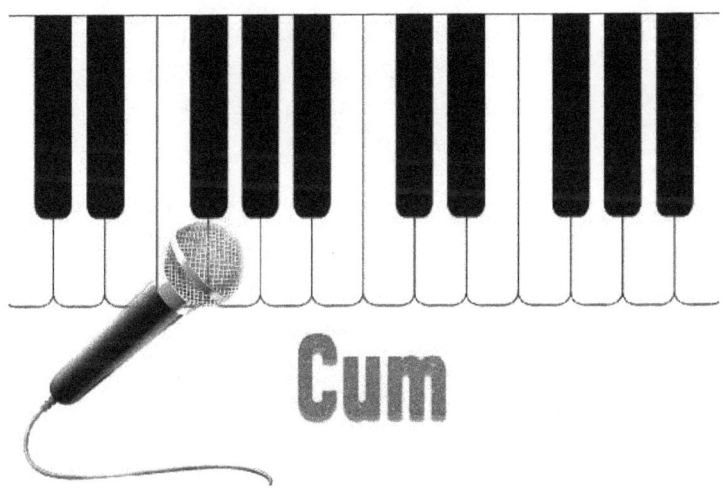

VERSE	Baby let me hold you let me pull you close, sending shivers up and down my spine down to my toes.
VERSE	Wanna kiss your body from head to toe, cover every inch - take it nice and slow.
VERSE	Baby bring your body down on top of me, temperature is risin' - baby can you feel my heat.
VERSE	Baby let me kiss you wanna suck your lips, lovin' the sensation going down below my clit.

VERSE	Baby let me feel it wanna taste your tongue, lovin' the sensation - wanna suck it when I cum.
VERSE	Love it when you suck and nibble my nipples, lovin' the sensation when you pull them .... that tickles.
VERSE	Baby wanna feel your body next to me, lovin' the sensation when you're makin' love to me.
VERSE	Baby feels so good deep inside of me, lovin' the sensation that your cock is givin' me.
VERSE	Baby feels so good give it all to me, do it good and hard gonna cum - shit - cum with me.
VERSE	Baby bring it to me wanna suck your cock, lovin' the sensation when you put it in my mouth.
VERSE	Lay me on my back and have a taste of me, lovin' the sensation when you're suckin' my pussy.
VERSE	Lie down on your back and take me for a ride, love it when you grab my ass and shove it deep inside.

VERSE	Rain is beating down against my window pane - baby, please - don't stop - I'm about to cum again.
VERSE	Baby hot and sweaty workin' overtime, lovin' the sensation when you take me from behind.

                        Repeat All

VERSE   As I sit and reminisce, I remember our first kiss. Oh, our feelings were so strong, and I knew our love had grown.

In the time I spent with you, we became much more than friends. Now we have something that's true, and I'm sure it never ends.

CHORUS   Don't you love me?
You know I'm always there.
Don't you love me?
You've got someone who cares.

CHANGE	My Love, I'm sincere. There's something special here. Don't you love me? Don't you love me? Don't you love me Dear?
VERSE	I will never forget all the roses that you've sent, all the places that I've been, all the people that I've met, all the dinners that we've had, the romance by candlelight, all the dancing until dawn with you holding me so tight...
CHORUS	Don't you love me? You know I'm always there. Don't you love me? You've got someone who cares.
CHANGE	My Love, I'm sincere. There's something special here... Don't you love me? Don't you love me? Don't you love me Dear?

I wasn't asking if he loved me – I was saying, "Aww... don't you love me?"

Joy & Pain – Life In The Key of Me

Every Time I Close My Eyes

VERSE   I fantasize about you when I'm sitting all alone. I dream it's you I'm talking to when I sit by the phone. I think of you when I'm at work and wish the day would end. 'Cause I know that when I get home we'll have more time to spend.

CHANGE   It's time for me to go to bed but something's on my mind. I want to close my eyes and sleep but rest is hard to find.

CHORUS   Every time I close my eyes I start to think of you, every time I close my eyes I dream of loving you.
Every time I close my eyes I start to think of you, every time I close my eyes I dream of loving you.

VERSE   My fantasies can take me anywhere I want to be. But fantasies cannot replace the love you give to me. I love to dream about you every day and every night. But dreams will never do for me - I want you in plain sight.

CHANGE   It's time for me to go to bed but something's on my mind. I want to close my eyes and sleep but rest is hard to find.

CHORUS   Every time I close my eyes I start to think of you, every time I close my eyes I dream of loving you.
Every time I close my eyes I start to think of you, every time I close my eyes I dream of loving you.

Repeat Chorus

Feeling Sexy

VERSE Seems like you're ready. I can see you out the corner of my eye. Rubbing my shoulder, you're touching me just the way I like – and if you wanna go down lower, we can get a quickie in – 'cause I got time. I just got out the shower – but if you wanna get it in...

CHANGE I can take another – 'cause I'm feeling sexy. 'Bout to change my mind. I ain't goin' nowhere. Tonight is our night...

CHORUS	Feeling Sexy! I'm 'bout to stay home! And put it on you! Feeling Sexy! I'm 'bout to stay home! And put it on you! Get wet! Get wet! Get wet! Get wet!
VERSE	I feel you rising so baby just bring your body here. It's perfect timing. Everyone's gone – no one will hear - and if you wanna go down lower, we can get a quickie in – 'cause I got time. I just got out the shower – but if you wanna get it in...
CHANGE	I can take another – 'cause I'm feeling sexy. 'Bout to change my mind. I ain't goin' nowhere. Tonight is our night...
CHORUS	Feeling Sexy! I'm 'bout to stay home! And put it on you! Feeling Sexy! I'm 'bout to stay home! And put it on you! Get wet! Get wet! Get wet! Get wet!

Joy & Pain – Life In The Key of Me

For A Long Time

VERSE I met you once by chance. Infatuation grew. I knew right then and there I wanted you. You took me by surprise, such kindness in your eyes. I asked myself, "How long can this be true?"

CHANGE The answer was quite clear. I knew you were sincere. I felt that I would always have you near.

CHORUS For a long time, I'm sure we'll be together. For a long time, I know it lasts forever. For a long time, I look into your eyes and now I see. For a long time, it will be you and me.

VERSE	I know you now so well. You're happy, I can tell. I feel this is the happiest I've been. I love you oh - so much. I need your loving touch. We have the kind of love that's hard to win.
CHANGE	With promises we made emotions never fade and we are one as long as our love stays.
CHORUS	For a long time, I'm sure we'll be together. For a long time, I know it lasts forever. For a long time, I look into your eyes and now I see. For a long time, it'll be you and me.

I wrote this when we first started dating. We've been together for 38 years, married for 20 years. I sure got this one right.

Joy & Pain – Life In The Key of Me

VERSE   Many times I've been down and out and I felt nobody cared. Then I'd call you on the telephone, and you say you'll be right there. Well I know I can count on' you to be there when I'm so blue and I know that you'll set me free from all my anxieties

CHANGE   I talked with all my friends - they said, "Girl, this won't last." I said, "No, no my friends it's not like in the past." This time I found someone - someone who's really true and that someone for me has sure got to be you 'cause we're...

CHORUS   HOT!! That's how I feel when we're together - HOT!!
HOT!! I haven't known anyone better - HOT!!

Repeat Verse, Change, Chorus

VERSE   You know you set me free from anxieties, I want you here with me. No matter what you do, I'm gonna get with you, tell you this much is true... Stop listenin' to my friends, don't matter if or when, this love will never end... You know you set me free from my anxieties, you know you set me freeeeeeeee... set me free.

Joy & Pain – Life In The Key of Me

How Can I?

VERSE	How can I go on living in this beautiful place? How can I go on living without you - not a trace? How can I see with these things happening?
CHORUS	How can I - tell me - how can I?
VERSE	How can I go on living without your touch? How can I go on - oh I'll miss you so much. How can I see with these things happening?
CHORUS	How can I - tell me - how can I?

CHANGE Do you know how it feels to find love is not real? Do you know what to say when your heart's in the way? Can you say in your mind, "She won't be there this time?" Can you be without me? Open your eyes, tell me...

CHORUS How can I - tell me - how can I?

VERSE How can I go on sleeping here every night? How can I go on when I know nothings right? How can I see with these things happening?

CHORUS How can I - tell me - how can I?

CHANGE Do you know how it feels to find love is not real? Do you know what to say when your heart's in the way? Can you say in your mind, "She won't be there this time?" Can you be without me open your eyes, tell me...

CHORUS How can I - tell me - how can I?

Joy & Pain – Life In The Key of Me

Heard Too Many Love Songs

VERSE   Once upon a time I had high hopes for you and me. Took some time to come to terms but now I finally see. You and I we never seem to talk about before. I guess I should now believe you don't love me no more.

CHANGE   Well I thought about advice I heard from my best friend. She says you'll come back to me but I say it's the end. She says listen to your heart 'cause love songs say it all. I say maybe I should read the writing on the wall.

CHORUS	I've heard too many love songs - they don't make everything all right. I've heard too many love songs - they just give me sleepless nights. I've heard too many love songs. I've heard too many love songs.
VERSE	Once upon a time I thought good things would come to pass. Looking back I see why our relationship won't last. You and I it seems we're at each other all the time. I wish I could go back to those days when you were mine.
CHANGE	I have had it, I'm fed up, and I can't stand the pain. All this bickering back and forth leaves nothing to be gained. I think I should feel in love that's how it's supposed to be. Listening to those love songs won't do anything for me.
CHORUS	I've heard too many love songs - they don't make everything all right. I've heard too many love songs - they just give me sleepless nights. I've heard too many love songs. I've heard too many love songs.

Joy & Pain – Life In The Key of Me

VERSE People say I'm in a daze whenever I'm with you. They say I'm blind, deaf and dumb; I don't know what to do. They say you're hurting me so much I won't open my eyes. They try to tell me you're no good - I tell them it's all lies.

CHANGE Maybe I should be afraid - there's a chance they're right. But I'd rather be with you to share your love tonight...

Joy & Pain – Life In The Key of Me

CHORUS   I don't want to wake up to find this love's not real. I can't help how I feel - I don't want to wake up. I don't want to wake up to find this love's not real. I can't help how I feel - I don't want to wake up.

VERSE   They try to tell me you're all wrong when I say that you're all right. They try to tell me to give up but I'll fight with all my might. I know just how I feel for you - won't let love slip away. I know you care about me too - let's bring love back today.

CHANGE   Maybe I should be afraid - there's a chance they're right. But I'd rather be with you to share your love tonight...

CHORUS   I don't want to wake up to find this love's not real. I can't help how I feel - I don't want to wake up. I don't want to wake up to find this love's not real. I can't help how I feel - I don't want to wake up.

I Don't Have What You Want

VERSE   You tossed him aside, then you chose to flaunt it. Now you won't speak to me 'cause I jumped up on it.

CHANGE   I chose the man, you chose to creep. I chose to love, you chose to cheat. Now you're so mad you won't even Speak!

CHORUS   I don't have what you want,
'Cause you didn't want it,
You didn't want it.
I don't have what you want,
'Cause you didn't want it.

Joy & Pain – Life In The Key of Me

VERSE You set yourself up for defeat.
I told you before – you can't beat the street.

CHANGE I chose the man, you chose to creep.
I chose to love, you chose to cheat.
Now you're so mad you won't even Speak!

CHORUS I don't have what you want,
'Cause you didn't want it,
You didn't want it.
I don't have what you want,
'Cause you didn't want it.

VERSE You mad? Bitch – so what? What the fuck you think I'd do? I kept tellin' you - stop fuckin' up! You wanna tell everybody I took your man – Bitch please! How could I take something you never had? It was all good when that cat you left with was beatin' your pussy every night but things changed when he switched up and started beatin' your face – now you wanna run back over here talkin' bout baby I want you back, please give me another chance – every time he gave you another chance he wound up in my arms and

on my shoulder – and since you left
he's wound up in my head, my heart,
and my bed... and I want to thank
you...

CHANGE I chose the man, you chose to creep.
I chose to love, you chose to cheat.
Now you're so mad you won't even
Speak!

CHORUS I don't have what you want,
'Cause you didn't want it,
You didn't want it.
I don't have what you want,
'Cause you didn't want it.

I Keep Holding On

VERSE   Any time I'm feeling I miss you
I close my eyes and I can be with
you. Instantly I recall what you do,
When we're making love – believe
it's true. As I close my eyes you're
here with me, making love to me
inspiringly, and...

CHORUS   I keep holding on.
(I can feel you touching me.)
I keep holding on.
(Now you're kissing my body.)
I keep holding on.
(Now you're licking up my thighs.)
I keep holding on.
(Now you're thrusting deep inside.)

VERSE	Seems so real as were both drenched in sweat. Feels so good but we're not finished yet. Now you're coming close, I'm getting wet. Keeping my eyes closed, but not there yet. You're on the top – the bottom excites me. I pull you close and now you're squeezing me, and...
CHORUS	I keep holding on. (I can feel you touching me.) I keep holding on. (Now you're kissing my body.) I keep holding on. (Now you're licking up my thighs.) I keep holding on. (Now you're thrusting deep inside.)

I Wanna Be Deep Inside Your Love

VERSE When I'm in your arms and I'm close to you I just feel so warm - you can feel it to. Right next to your heart where I want to be, feeling so in love I'm in ecstasy.

CHORUS I wanna be deep inside your love.
I wanna be deep inside your love.
I wanna be deep inside your love.
I wanna be deep inside your love.

VERSE   When the lights are dim and we're dancing slow, I feel so content I want you to know. There's a special bond when were close like this and when morning comes I can reminisce.

CHORUS   I wanna be deep inside your love.
         I wanna be deep inside your love.
         I wanna be deep inside your love.
         I wanna be deep inside your love.

CHORUS   I wanna be deep inside your love.
         I wanna be deep inside your love.
         I wanna be deep inside your love.
         I wanna be deep inside your love.

VERSE   When we are together we have such a nice time, but baby when you leave me I can't get you off my mind. And when I dream about you it's the perfect fantasy, but baby when I wake up it won't be reality.

CHANGE   Without a real commitment I won't be satisfied. I won't settle for less anymore - I have tried...

Joy & Pain – Life In The Key of Me

CHORUS   I just want to be there in the morning light. I just want to be there - we can share the night. I just want to be there when the moment's right. I just want to be there.

VERSE   You have changed my feelings and I really love you. I think about us always and I hope you do too. It's time for us to move on - we're not playing anymore. I want to get together 'cause it's not like before.

CHANGE   Without a real commitment I won't be satisfied. I won't settle for less anymore - I have tried...

CHORUS   I just want to be there in the morning light. I just want to be there - we can share the night. I just want to be there when the moment's right. I just want to be there.

Joy & Pain – Life In The Key of Me

VERSE   Come to me and you will see how much I care for you. Give me a chance to show you now - I swear I won't hurt you.

CHANGE Open your eyes and you will see how much you really mean to me. Just when you think all hope is gone, then you'll find out you're not alone.

CHORUS Look at me... Look at me...

Joy & Pain – Life In The Key of Me

VERSE   Find yourself a friend in me 'cause I'm in love with you. In your heart there's so much pain – I'll take it all from you.

CHANGE   Open your eyes and you will see how much you really mean to me. Just when you think all hope is gone, then you'll find out you're not alone.

CHORUS   Look at me... Look at me...

VERSE   I remember when you used to want me to hold your hand. I remember when you used to want me to understand.

CHANGE   I remember when we talked about and thought about each other. I remember when the stars were out, just you and I, no other.

CHORUS   I remember when...
I remember when...

VERSE I remember when you used to tell me you love me so. I remember when you used to tell me you won't let go.

CHANGE I remember when you said to me, "We'll always be together."
I remember when you said to me, "We'll be in love forever."

CHORUS I remember when...
I remember when...

CHANGE I remember when you looked at me and you could see I loved you. I remember when you used to see the best in me was with you.

CHORUS I remember when...
I remember when...

I Want You Out Now!

VERSE Yes, that's right - I want you out now! You know, things used to be so good between us. Unhappiness was hard to find. Yea, Baby I remember when we used to go for walks together holding hands, kissing, hugging, touching. But that was a long, long time ago. I can't remember when the last time was ... no - I'm not crying - you know I have allergies - don't even try it! Yea, you just knew I wouldn't get over you didn't you? Promising me you'd be faithful and true when the only thing you were ever faithful and true to was your reputation as a gigolo - oh, did you think I wouldn't find out about that? Like I said - I want you out now!

VERSE	Yea, you used to tell me how much you loved me and needed me. Do you remember the last thing you did for me? I'll never forget - it was the day you asked me to marry you. My ring was too small so I took it to the jewelers to have it cut - you know what I felt like in front of everybody when he said I'd do better buying the real thing. It was a beautiful ceremony considering the fact that you left me standing at the altar. They never did understand why I still wanted the tape of our ceremony - one that didn't happen - you see, I thought I would go home and watch my wedding - not my rejection. Like I said - I want you out now!

VERSE Oh - by the way - when you leave? Just let the door knob hit you where the good Lord spit you - 'cause as far as I'm concerned, you're not worth the tears - at least not mine anyway. Yes, I want my keys - I can't trust you to throw them out. And don't even think that you can take the car, the house, the credit cards, or the money - No you can't BORROW anything for a cab - do the best you can!

LOL! NO! This isn't a true story! I was up late, I started scribbling, and this came out!

I Want You So Bad

VERSE   I've loved you since the day I saw you. I tried to tell you. You just pushed me away. And yesterday I came to see you to be with you but you told me not to stay.

CHANGE   You'll never how much I need you. You'll never know how much I care. You never ever let me be with you. You never gave me a chance. Not a chance.

CHORUS   I want you. I need you. I love you. I want you so bad.
I want you. I need you. I love you. I want you so bad.

Joy & Pain – Life In The Key of Me

VERSE   When love finds you broken hearted, there is a place where you can let your guard down. When you find that she's departed you can come here – 'cause I'll always be 'round.

CHANGE   Give me a chance and you will see. It's so easy to trust me. It's okay – I won't hurt you, 'cause I know what you've been through...

CHORUS I Will Be There. I will be there – ready and waiting. I Will Be There. For your love, don't be mistaken. I Will Be There. I will be there when you need me. I Will Be There. When you need me that's where I'll be.

VERSE When love finds you broken hearted, there is a place where you can let your guard down. When you find that she's departed you can come here – 'cause I'll always be 'round.

CHANGE Give me a chance and you will see. It's so easy to trust me. It's okay – I won't hurt you, 'cause I know what you've been through...

CHORUS I Will Be There. I will be there – ready and waiting. I Will Be There. For your love, don't be mistaken. I Will Be There. I will be there when you need me. I Will Be There. When you need me that's where I'll be.

Joy & Pain – Life In The Key of Me

VERSE   Don't need your money 'cause a platinum card can buy most anything from trips around the world to diamond, platinum rings...

CHORUS Can I Git A Ride?
(Ride that dick won't cha let me?)
Baby, come inside.
(Ride that dick won't cha let me?)
Are you ready yet?
(Ride that dick won't cha let me?)
'Cause I'm moist & wet.
(Ride that dick won't cha let me?)
Baby le'me see
(Ride that dick won't cha let me?)
what's in store for me.
(Ride that dick won't cha let me?)

What cha gonna do?
(Ride that dick won't cha let me?)
It's all up to you.
(Ride that dick won't cha let me?)

VERSE Don't wanna go to a restaurant 'cause I already ate. I got that movie on DVD – besides – it's getting late...

CHORUS Can I Git A Ride?
(Ride that dick won't cha let me?)
Baby, come inside.
(Ride that dick won't cha let me?)
Are you ready yet?
(Ride that dick won't cha let me?)
'Cause I'm moist & wet.
(Ride that dick won't cha let me?)
Baby le'me see
(Ride that dick won't cha let me?)
what's in store for me.
(Ride that dick won't cha let me?)
What cha gonna do?
(Ride that dick won't cha let me?)
It's all up to you.
(Ride that dick won't cha let me?)

Joy & Pain – Life In The Key of Me

Just A Dream

VERSE When I was young I used to think that love was nothing new. I thought about the things you said the day that I met you. We started out with something real and promises were made. But now I find the love we share has somehow come to fade.

CHANGE As time went on, you were not there - where did our love go wrong, or don't you care - maybe you felt this coming all along. How could you look me in my eyes and not be straight with me? Let's talk about it - please don't take your love away from me!

Joy & Pain – Life In The Key of Me

CHORUS   It was just a dream - how can I go on? It was just a dream - how can I be strong? It was just a dream - how could I have known? It was just a dream. It was just a dream.

VERSE   I used to think you cared enough to be here day and night. Now all I do is wait for you and wish that things were right. I never thought that you and I would someday see the end. I wish that we could talk things out and start over again.

CHANGE   As time went on, you were not there - where did our love go wrong, or don't you care - maybe you felt this coming all along. How could you look me in my eyes and not be straight with me? Let's talk about it - please don't take your love away from me!

CHORUS   It was just a dream - how can I go on? It was just a dream - how can I be strong? It was just a dream - how could I have known? It was just a dream. It was just a dream.

VERSE   How can I go on without you? What do you expect me to do? This is not how our love should be. Why are you doing this to me when you know I gave you my heart and I loved you right from the start? If I could just have one last wish, we would never end up like this.

Joy & Pain – Life In The Key of Me

VERSE   Lovin' at first sight, lovin' me alright. Lovin' even when things ain't goin' right. Lovin' me all night 'till the mornin' light...

CHORUS   Love Me Baby

VERSE   Lovin' me in spite of my many faults. Lovin' through the hurt, breakin' down my walls. Lovin' on my heart, kissin' all my scars...

CHORUS   Love Me Baby

Joy & Pain – Life In The Key of Me

VERSE	Lovin' every day when I've lost my way. Lovin' me is hard, don't know what to say. Lovin' let's me know that you wanna stay...
CHORUS	Love Me Baby
VERSE	Lovin' me in spite of it being hot. Lovin' all the while even when I'm not. Lovin' in the dark 'till you find the spot...
CHORUS	Love Me Baby
VERSE	Lovin' how you touch, and I'm feelin' good. Lovin' by my side like I knew you could. Lovin' all along 'till I understood...
CHORUS	Love Me Baby

Joy & Pain – Life In The Key of Me

VERSE

I don't know how you got here - but I'm glad you came. I've had feelings before - but it's not the same. This is all too familiar - but not like before. And although I deny it - I know I need more.

CHANGE

I went through all the motions - threw away the key. But you still found a way - reached inside of me. Should I follow my heart - or walk out the door. My mind is telling me noooooooooo but...

CHORUS	My Heart Says Yes!
My Heart Says Yes!
My Heart Says Yes! To you!
	My Heart Says Yes!
My Heart Says Yes!
My Heart Says Yes!
My Heart Says Yes!
VERSE	I'm not sure what I'm doing - but it feels so right. In a state of confusion - feelings I can't fight. I'm beginning to wonder - could you be the one. I think you've started something that can't be undone.
CHANGE	I went through all the motions - threw away the key. But you still found a way - reached inside of me. Should I follow my heart - or walk out the door. My mind is telling me nooooooooooo... Telling me nooooooooo but...
CHORUS	My Heart Says Yes!
My Heart Says Yes!
My Heart Says Yes! To you!

My Heart Says Yes!
My Heart Says Yes!
My Heart Says Yes!
My Heart Says Yes!

This song was entered into the very first American Idol Songwriter's Competition in 2007.

Joy & Pain – Life In The Key of Me

VERSE   There are times in my life when love brings to my mind fantasies that I wish I could change. And although I insist in my heart this is it I know deep down things won't stay the same.

CHANGE   Now I can't push my feelings aside - what I feel I can't hide - it's the wrong thing to do.

CHORUS   Now I won't give up on you.

             Repeat Verse, Change, Chorus

Joy & Pain – Life In The Key of Me

VERSE
: Walking down the street holding hands with the one I love. Feeling so romantic, gazing at the stars above.

CHANGE
: Sometimes I feel the need to show how much I really care. And when I kiss your lips I know romance is in the air.

CHORUS
: And people watch us kissing. They can watch all they want to. People watch us kissing. I don't care because I love you.

Repeat Verse, Change, Chorus

People Change – Why Can't We?

VERSE   Why do we fight each night? Why can't we make things right? Why did love slip away? Why should we end this way?

CHANGE   Can't you see how I feel? What went wrong - it's unreal. Tell me how love should be?

CHORUS   People change - why can't we?

VERSE   I don't know what to do. I am sure I've lost you. I need you can't you see? I love you - why hurt me?

CHANGE	Can't you see how I feel? What went wrong - it's unreal. Tell me how love should be?
CHORUS	People change - why can't we?
VERSE	How did we come so far unhappy as we are? What can we do for now? Let's make this work somehow.
CHANGE	Can't you see how I feel? What went wrong - it's unreal. Tell me how love should be?
CHORUS	People change - why can't we?

VERSE   Never felt this way before and I'm not ashamed. Everyone around can see you're the one to blame. Wrap your arms around me darlin' - I'm in ecstasy. Tonight I want us to create the perfect fantasy.

CHANGE I'm gonna take you and I hope that you're prepared. 'Cause where we're goin' can never be compared. I want you and I know that you want me. When we get together, we'll make history because you're....

Joy & Pain – Life In The Key of Me

CHORUS Sweeter than a sugar plum,
Sexy Chocolate
And I'm gonna get me some,
Sexy Chocolate
Sweeter than a lollipop,
Sexy Chocolate
Tasty down to the last drop,
Sexy Chocolate

VERSE Looking forward to the time we can be alone. Hurry, come to me my love, disconnect the phone. Hunger for your touch my darlin' - I'm filled with desire! You ignite this passion, now come put out the fire!

CHANGE I'm gonna take you and I hope that you're prepared. 'Cause where we're goin' can never be compared. I want you and I know that you want me. When we get together, we'll make history because you're....

Joy & Pain – Life In The Key of Me

CHORUS
Sweeter than a sugar plum,
Sexy Chocolate
And I'm gonna get me some,
Sexy Chocolate
Sweeter than a lollipop,
Sexy Chocolate
Tasty down to the last drop,
Sexy Chocolate

VERSE
Pull me closer to your body, wanna taste your lips. Lay me down and work it baby, grab hold of my hips. Slide yourself between my thighs right where I want it. Give me every inch of your sexy chocolate.

CHANGE
I'm gonna take you and I hope that you're prepared. 'Cause where we're goin' can never be compared. I want you and I know that you want me. When we get together, we'll make history because you're....

CHORUS   Sweeter than a sugar plum,
          Sexy Chocolate
          And I'm gonna get me some,
          Sexy Chocolate
          Sweeter than a lollipop,
          Sexy Chocolate
          Tasty down to the last drop,
          Sexy Chocolate

CHORUS   Sweet Sexy Chocolate
          Feels so good to me baby,
          Sexy Chocolate
          Tasty, and sexy
          Sexy Chocolate
          And sweet, Sexy Chocolate

VERSE As I sit here alone.
(So lost without you babe.)
I'm not sure what went wrong
(So lost without you babe.)
I just can't understand
(So lost without you babe.)
how things got out of hand.
(So lost without you babe.)

CHANGE I'm so numb I don't feel.
Can't accept this is real.
I don't know how to stand.
Without you I don't know who I am.

CHANGE   And I, I feel like my well has run dry! And I have such pain that I can't even cry! And I can't live without you in my life!

CHANGE   Can't you see you're the best part of me?

VERSE   I don't sleep. I can't eat.
(So lost without you babe.)
Still feel you in my dreams.
(So lost without you babe.)
Walk around in a daze
(So lost without you babe.)
when I hear love songs play.
(So lost without you babe.)

CHANGE   I'm so numb I don't feel.
Can't accept this is real.
I don't know how to stand.
Without you I don't know who I am.

CHANGE   And I, I feel like my well has run dry! And I have such pain that I can't even cry! And I can't live without you in my life!

CHANGE   Can't you see you're the best part of me?

Joy & Pain – Life In The Key of Me

Taste of Honey

VERSE   I don't understand this situation. I don't really have an explanation. But if you were in my shoes, you wouldn't blame me.

VERSE   You say you hold me accountable. You say you hold me responsible. But I don't need help so please don't try to save me.

CHANGE   When I'm with you my heart's on fire. You're the only one I desire. You could bring me to my knees. I'd do anything you please.

CHORUS	When it comes to your love baby, it's like having a taste of honey! A taste is just a tease - I need to have the whole jar! When it comes to your love baby, it's like having a taste of honey! A taste is just a tease - I need to have the whole jar!
VERSE	You won't ever have to ask the question. I can give you more than just affection. But if you won't let me in, how can I show it. All I ask is you give me a try and you'll never have to wonder why. But if you won't open up, you'll never know it.
CHANGE	When I'm with you my heart's on fire. You're the only one I desire. You could bring me to my knees. I'd do anything you please.
CHORUS	When it comes to your love baby, it's like having a taste of honey! A taste is just a tease - I need to have the whole jar! When it comes to your love baby, it's like having a taste of honey! A taste is just a tease - I need to have the whole jar!

Joy & Pain – Life In The Key of Me

That's How You Find Love

VERSE When you walk through the park and someone special looks your way. When you look in his eyes and you can't find the right words to say.

CHORUS That's how you find love.

VERSE When you feel all mixed up because he walked by you just can't wait. When he tells you good night and you wonder how much more you can take.

CHORUS That's how you find love.

CHANGE	That's how you find love in your heart every day, every night, 'cause you know you feel it down in your heart and soul where your feelings will flow and his love will follow you forever.
CHORUS	That's how you find love.
VERSE	When your feelings are strong and you see him in a different light. When you want to go on, and you lay dreaming of him at night.
CHORUS	That's how you find love.
VERSE	When your heart opens up and you finally show him how much you care. When you know love is true and you both have special love you can share.
CHORUS	That's how you find love.
	Repeat Change, Chorus

Thanks For The Love

VERSE   It's Christmas time again and soon we will exchange our gifts. But something's on my mind I want to tell you - I insist. Each year I want to give you something better than before; not something you can buy but something that means so much more. So I wrote you this song to tell you how much I love you, and I wrote you this song, 'cause I want to say this to you...

CHORUS   Thanks for the love you've given me. Thanks for the love, makes me happy.

CHANGE   With everything you do this song will remind you of our love.

VERSE   Each year we do our best to show each other that we care. We decorate the tree and give out presents everywhere. We help our families and spend time with our closest friends. We toast to the New Year and know our love will never end. So I wrote you this song to tell you how much I love you, and I wrote you this song 'cause I want to say this to you...

CHORUS   Thanks for the love you've given me. Thanks for the love, makes me happy.

CHANGE   With everything ng you do this song will remind you of our love.

Joy & Pain – Life In The Key of Me

True Love

VERSE   Being in love with you is all that I want to do. Needing you more each day, feeling a special way.

CHANGE   I'm finding it hard to be. Without you I just can't see. You're on my mind all the time. I've found what's so hard to find...

CHORUS   'Cause I find true love whenever I'm with you love and I know that with your love my heart will sing. 'Cause I find true love whenever I'm with you love and I know you can make love a special thing.

VERSE   Missing you all the time, wishing that you were mine. Seeing you more and more, closer now than before.

CHANGE   I'm finding it hard to be. Without you I just can't see. You're on my mind all the time. I've found what's so hard to find...

CHORUS   'Cause I find true love whenever I'm with you love and I know that with your love my heart will sing. 'Cause I find true love whenever I'm with you love and I know you can make love a special thing.

Joy & Pain – Life In The Key of Me

You Don't Like Me Any More

VERSE I don't know what went wrong. I keep asking myself, "Was it me all along?" I don't know what to say. Am I dreaming this or do you feel the same way.

CHANGE I just can't stand the pain. Arguing is insane. What have I done to you? Tell me - what can I do?

CHORUS You don't like me any more. I can see it in your eyes - it's not like before. You don't like me any more. What I see here is something that I can't ignore. You don't like me any more. You don't like me any more.

VERSE	I don't know where I stand. All the problems between us are far out of hand. I can't figure it out. When we try to talk all we can do is shout.
CHANGE	Now we're strangers - that's sad. Where's the love that we had? After all we've been through? How come I never knew?
CHORUS	You don't like me any more. I can see it in your eyes - it's not like before. You don't like me any more. What I see here is something ng that I can't ignore. You don't like me any more. You don't like me any more.

LOL! My husband used to tell me I sounded like I was yelling whenever I sang this song.

Joy & Pain – Life In The Key of Me

You Make Me Feel Good Inside

VERSE My love, I realize I've hurt you deeply in the past. I know that what we have is much too good - let's make it last. Well I tried so hard to make you see all the things you really do for me, but I guess you couldn't take it any more...

CHANGE Well I talked with all my friends and they said I've been unkind. They said I'd only hurt you more but I said, "No - not this time." I realize I need your love and I've sure made up my mind...

CHORUS	'Cause loving you is easy, and I want you to be with me 'cause you make me feel good inside.
VERSE	And now I know for sure just what I've lost - I want you back. I know I love you more now than before and that's a fact. Well I tried so hard to make you see all the things you really do for me, but I guess you couldn't take it any more...
CHANGE	Well I talked with all my friends and they said I've been unkind. They said I'd only hurt you more but I said, "No - not this time." I realize I need your love and I've sure made up my mind...
CHORUS	'Cause loving you is easy, and I want you to be with me 'cause you make me feel good inside.

Joy & Pain – Life In The Key of Me

VERSE   You told me that you love me and wanted your life with me. You made these promises and didn't mean it. You said we'd be together and love would last forever, but something else went wrong - I didn't see it.

CHANGE   You had lots of time - more than you deserved. Now you want me back. Boy, you've got some nerve.

CHORUS	Don't look for second chanes. Don't wonder where romance is. You blew it this time baby, you blew it. Don't try to reason why. Don't ask for one more try. You blew it this time baby, you blew it.
VERSE	I waited for a long time and thought one day you'd be mine. I hoped that our marriage was your intention. Each time we talked it over you wanted to go slower. I guess that I just had the wrong impression.
CHANGE	You had lots of time - more than you deserved. Now you want me back. Boy, you've got some nerve.
CHORUS	Don't look for second chances. Don't wonder where romance is. You blew it this time baby, you blew it. Don't try to reason why. Don't ask for one more try. You blew it this time baby, you blew it.

You Were Just In Time

VERSE — There was a time when I was feeling very low. You came into my life and loved me even though you knew that someone special was keeping us apart and yet you waited for me until you won my heart.

CHANGE — I used to think true love could never be. I never knew that you'd be there for me.

CHORUS — You were just in time, a friend who would be kind. You were just in time, the best friend I could find. You were just in time. You were just in time.

VERSE	I feel as though I've been there so many times before, and each time love is better. I guess I'll try once more. I've known you for a long time. It's clear enough to see that you are someone special and that's enough for me.
CHANGE	I used to think true love could never be. I never knew that you'd be there for me.
CHORUS	You were just in time, a friend who would be kind. You were just in time, the best friend I could find. You were just in time. You were just in time.

www.ingramcontent.com/pod-product-compliance
Lightning Source LLC
Chambersburg PA
CBHW032005060426
42449CB00031B/516